LET'S SHARE A HOPE STORY

SHAWNTA SMITH SAYNER

With an approach dedicated to supporting self-love, self-care, diversity, and inclusion, the Let's Share series empowers us to communicate, care, and connect!
Collect them all!

For you
(yes, you!)

There will always be people

who care about you.

They will be there,
whatever you think, say, or do.

And however you look,
and whomever you love,

And whenever you met,
and wherever you're from,

And the language you speak,
and the home where you live,

The way your body works,
and your color of skin,

Your customs and choices —
and the entire lot,

Your interests and hobbies,
what you like and do not.

There are as many beliefs
as there are people.

Each one is unique
and not always so simple.

There are also people
who you may come to face,

That might treat you with
mistrust, suspicion, and hate,

Because you are different
from the people they know,

And they could be confused
about how they should show,

Their own challenging feelings
around something new,

And they could make choices
that are unkind to you.

Whoever you are
on the inside and outside,

Why you look how you look
or what you abide by,

You are so very special
and never alone,

Though it can seem that way
when our feelings sink low.

It is sure there is no one exactly like you,

But there are other people out in the world who,

Can share so much with you, in the most awesome ways.

If you don't know them yet, you will find them someday!

Try to love who you love —
and then love even more,

Bring respect and kindness
to everyone's door.

There is always the chance
it may not be returned,

But each setback can offer
a lesson to learn.

You must never let go
of those pieces of you,

That know just what you feel
and believe to be true,

But remember there's room
for some different folks, too,

Who might also have
values much like you do —

Like treating others
how they want to be treated.

(Not only the way that we think may be needed.)

What makes you the best you,
and makes you so special,

Is worth sharing with those
who will help you be well,

That will stand by your side,
and can help you feel safe.

(Whether one friend or many, can be just as great.)

We can all learn to love
at least little bits more,

With each passing day than
we were able before.

Together is a wonderful
way to succeed,

To grow, thrive, and connect —
to help others in need.

Prepare love and respect
for whomever you meet;

It is free to be given
and priceless received.

And of course don't forget
to save some for yourself!

(All too often we don't do that nearly enough.)

For somebody somewhere loves
you more than you know.

(I bet more than you realize are loving you so!)

Make sure you hold dearly
every single last one –

Each second of each day
of each year and beyond.

It's okay to feel lonely,
but now you must see...

You were never alone,

Shawnta Smith Sayner is an educator, caregiver, and lifelong learning advocate who supports students, faculty, and families alike, working in schools and traveling as a guest speaker. Known for *WeAreTeachers'* "15 Ways to Bring More Positive Language into Your Classroom and School," Shawnta's passions extend to supporting wellness, diversity, and inclusion throughout communities. Shawnta lives with her beautifully multicultural family near Milwaukee, WI.

Also by Shawnta Smith Sayner:
Let's Share a Hair Story
Let's Share a Superhero Story
Let's Share a Holiday Story

For freebies, updates, and more, please visit www.shawntasmithsayner.com.

Copyright © 2020 by Shawnta Smith Sayner

All rights reserved. Published by Inclusive Books & More, Brookfield, WI. No part of this publication may be reproduced, stored in a retrieval system, or transmitted in any form or by any means, electronic, mechanical, photocopying, recording, or otherwise, without written permission of the copyright holder. For information regarding permission, contact the publisher through its website: www.inclusivebooksandmore.com.

This book is a work of creative nonfiction. Names, characters, places, and incidents are either the product of the author's imagination or are used fictitiously. Any resemblance to actual persons, living or dead, business establishments, events, or locales is entirely coincidental.

Library of Congress Cataloging-in-Publication Data available / Library of Congress Control Number: 2020916882
ISBN: 978-1-952944-10-9 (hc) / ISBN: 978-1-952944-04-8 (pb) / ISBN: 978-1-952944-05-5 (eb)

First Edition: September 2020

www.ingramcontent.com/pod-product-compliance
Lightning Source LLC
Chambersburg PA
CBHW050752110526
44592CB00002B/42